BORIE

Adolphe Borie: "Tulips"

ADOLPHE BORIE

GEORGE BIDDLE

1937

THE AMERICAN FEDERATION OF ARTS, WASHINGTON

FORMAT BY HARRY ROBERTS, JR. · COMPOSITION & LETTER-PRESS BY THE JOHN D. LUCAS PRINTING CO., BALTIMORE · ENGRAVINGS BY THE STANDARD ENGRAVING CO., WASHINGTON · BINDING BY THE F. J. HOWARD CO., BALTIMORE · PAPER: FOR PLATES, BY DILL & COLLINS, PHILADELPHIA; FOR TEXT, BY THE LINWEAVE ASSOCIATION, SPRINGFIELD

LIST OF ILLUSTRATIONS

CHRONOLOGY

1877

Born in Philadelphia (*January 5*).

1895

Graduated from Lawrenceville School.

1895-1896

Spent at the University of Pennsylvania.

1896-1899

Studied at the Pennsylvania Academy of Fine Arts under Chase and Anschutz.

1899-1902

Studied under Carl Marr at the Royal Academy in Munich. Among his fellow students were Frederick Clay Bartlett, Carroll Tyson, Joseph Pearson, and Henry Rittenberg. Occasional visits to Paris and Vienna.

1902

Returned to Philadelphia.

1905

Failure of family bank.

1907

Married Edith Pettit. Spent a year in Paris. Exhibited in the Salon des Beaux-Arts.

1908-1915

Spent in Philadelphia. Studio in Washington Square until 1911.

1910

Beck Gold Medal for Portraiture at Pennsylvania Academy of Fine Arts.

1910

Summer in Italy.

1911

Bought the house at 4100 Pine Street, Philadelphia. Summer in Scotland.

1912

Went to Wyoming in the spring and stayed there until November.

1913

Peter born.

1915

Silver Medal Panama-Pacific Exhibition, San Francisco. Exhibition of his work at the Folsom Gallery, New York.

1915-1919

Lived in New York.

1916-1919

Spent the summers working at Ogunquit, Maine, where were also Karfiol, Hamilton Easter Field, the sculptor Laurent, and Niles Spencer.

1917

Maynard Portrait Prize, National Academy. Associate Member of National Academy.

1917

After the entrance of the United States into the war, worked for a year at camouflaging ships, and in 1918 did portraits in various mediums in return for subscriptions to the last Liberty Loan.

1919-1921

Back in Philadelphia.

1921-1924

Returned to Paris. Studio at 84 rue d'Assas.

1924-1934

Lived at 4100 Pine Street.

1926

Silver Medal, Sesqui-Centennial Exhibition, Philadelphia.
Third Clark Prize and Corcoran Bronze Medal at Corcoran Gallery, Washington.

1926

Summer in Portugal and Spain.

1928

Gold Medal, Philadelphia Art Club.
Norman Wait Harris Bronze Medal, Art Institute of Chicago.

1929

Summer in Germany and Paris.

1931

Summer in Italy, Paris, and Ireland.

1933

Summer in Mexico.

1934

In April made full Academician of National Academy.

1934

Died at 4100 Pine Street, after a short attack of pneumonia, at the age of fifty-seven (*May 14*).

ADOLPHE BORIE

I.

THE WINTER of 1934 was long and harsh. There was a terrific blizzard late in February and by the end of March the frost still lay deep in the ground. Consequently, toward the middle of April the forsythias were just out and a magnolia tree in full bud could be glimpsed above a gray stucco garden wall on the corner of Forty-first and Pine Streets in West Philadelphia.

There Adolphe Borie died with the sudden, ruthless, irrational tragedy of life, a month later, with spring still in the air.

To me he was a friend, an artist, and a brother. In varying degrees of relationship he was exactly that to all Philadelphia painters, younger and contemporary alike. And I think his greatest contribution—apart from his own work—was that easy, human, intimate, but always intense, interest and participation in the art of his city and his fellow artists. We shall never have valid, honest, regional art in America without this intimate, traditional participation by our artists. Borie was loved during his lifetime. The value of his contribution was understood with a shock upon his death.

I met Adolphe in 1911, coming to him with the drowning earnestness of a novice, much awed, dedicated to a high purpose, ready to squeeze with numberless questions every drop from this precious fruit. He took it all—no doubt with a certain sly delight—with his usual cosmopolitan and friendly urbanity. I must let him give me a letter to Mary Cassatt, who is probably still at Grasse with Renoir, and who can introduce me to Degas when she is back in her Paris apartment. And I should drop in on Fred Frieseke, who will know what is going on in Paris and can have me put up at the American Art Club. Yes, he had seen the work of Matisse and Picasso, and he envied me a winter in Paris just now. No, he agreed with me of course that Munich was probably not as good a place to study as when he had been there. And how about another high-ball, if you don't think the weather too hot? No, the full length painting of Edith is by the sculptor Mac-Monnies, commissioned by her father, two years before our marriage. I understand MacMonnies has a studio at Giverny now, and by the way if you're near Paris next summer the place might just suit you.

I loved him from that moment, intoxicated by his charm, by that rare sympathy, or understanding, or intelligence with which he actually enjoyed talking to an art student as to a friend and equal.

With Borie, as with all artists, there was a certain tangible relation between his work and his physical and inner being. In every sense he was an aristocrat—in looks, manners, grooming, and social background—and that manner he carried with the same ease and detachment with which he painted. An envious friend once said of him, "He seems better dressed in old clothes, better groomed with an unshaved beard, more punctilious lounging in a chair, than anyone else in the room." His almost studied ease and manner were, I think, the outward, visible sign of an inner graciousness which characterizes all nature's born aristocrats. But the essence of his charm was the warmth of his friendship and his almost feminine desire to please, never to bore. It was this will to understand and to reciprocate which he held like a shield before him, to conceal from the world the doubts, the inner probings, the moods, dejection, disappointments, the conceit, the pride, the ego of the artist. And so he was liked by all, by the conservative, fox-hunting, eighteenth-century Tories of the Main Line, by the professional models, by the French, Italian, or English artists and men of letters whom he met in Europe or who drifted through the rangy hospitality which he and Edith dispensed at 4100 Pine, by young artists whom he helped, by the dullard trustees of the Pennsylvania Academy of Fine Arts, by the cowboys of Wyoming, by fragile Charleston spinsters, by one and all of the packers, freighters, truckmen, icemen, and bootleggers with whom he had occasion to deal. Yes, he was liked by all; and, giving more than he asked for in return, was understood by few.

His fancy was whimsical, gently Rabelaisian, boyishly naughty, dreading sentimentality yet always sunny and warm. He could pick any commonplace from one's mouth and instantly clothe it with just the needed touch, toss it in the air, enlarge it to the grotesque, and suddenly come down to earth with his young enthusiasm, disdainful only of pedantry and dullness.

Once I had sent him my model, Nell, who for professional purposes had asked me for the loan of an evening dress. "Go to Borie," I had suggested, "he is a married man and doubtless has a fine collection of really handsome gowns." He later described her visit. She came impetuously, toward sundown, and stated her mission; and then, as if realizing her social obligations, added, "But, Mr. Borie, I am surely disturbing you and your wife at your evening meal!" No, it was quite all right, and he brought her in and opened to her the wealth of his chest of costumes. Entranced, she could not make up her mind and finally turned toward him with a flush of liquid candor. "I am only a poor working girl and have never worn an evening gown. But tell me, you that have seen me stark naked, should I wear a square neck or a V?"

As a professional portrait painter he was, of course, subjected to the petty family criticisms and sartorial strictures of his clients. This side of his work, which was a living gall to him, he would sublimate in a savage drollery. "I feel just like a fashionable tailor at the final fitting. Today there was a *post-mortem* and the family were delighted with the face. But the coat had to be re-cut. I took it in at the waist, put some padding in the shoulders, and finally achieved the right note by substituting a pearl gray Charvet cravat for a Christmas-sale necktie from Wanamaker's. '*And*,' he said, 'as I chalked the alterations on the canvas, I could feel my mouth bristling with pins.' "

At another time he described to me the painter X, whose sweeping brush strokes, whose turmoil of color, the fury of whose execution, he had as a Munich student vastly admired. "One day I came upon him painting," he said, "it was a mellow spring day in the mountains of Garmisch-Partenkirchen. X sat on a high stool, bespectacled, swathed in mufflers, encased in galoshes and woolen mittens, cold drops pearling from his eyes and nose. With a fine camel's hair brush he was laboriously building up a gigantic brush stroke. And he was still working on the same brush stroke four days later. . . . That," he added, "seemed to be the consummation of art, a symbol of the triumph of spirit over matter."

ADOLPHE AND his wife, Edith Pettit, were both of French Catholic stock. The original American progenitor, Jean Borie, was born at Villeneuve-sur-Lot, in Gascony, where his father had been a ship-owner who traded from Bordeaux. Sailing on one of his father's ships in 1802, he was caught in the bloody insurrection in Haiti and escaped as best he could from Dessaline's wrath. He made his way to Philadelphia where he married Sophie Beauveau, whose father, Jean Pierre Hyacinthe Beauveau, was also a French ship-owner, born on St. Vincent. Beauveau traded among the West Indies and was, like Borie, caught in the Haitian rebellion, from which he escaped to the hills with his wife and their four daughters. Here he died of yellow fever, but the others were able to take passage secretly to Philadelphia.

In Philadelphia Jean Borie lived on with Sophie and apparently prospered, since he founded the wine business of Borie and Bohlen and begat thirteen children. His son, Adolphe, developed the wine business into a bank. And it was for a career in this family banking business that his great-nephew was destined. Many of Adolphe's youthful escapades were perhaps a subconscious revolt against a contraction of his artist's joy in living. His stays at various schools were brief and he ended his career at the University of Pennsylvania in a halo of undergraduate respect by coaxing and dragging one night an ancient cart horse up the four flights of his dormitory stairs. The finally successful efforts of the Dean and the fire department to wheedle down to earth the startled and outraged animal must have been to them a long nightmare.

He could visualize himself with playful drollery. "I am a real cockney and like every city dweller adore the mirage of bucolic happiness. My hunger for the country is satisfied with a picnic once a year in the Wissahickon Park. I can lie on my back, or hunt for four leaf clovers, and perhaps visualize a little farm by the Susquehanna, raising chickens and growing my own vegetables. About four o'clock I am satiated with nature and taxi back to the city, shake up some cocktails, and feel, thank God, that for months at least I have well purged the country from my system."

I wish I could describe the quiet, leisurely, roomy Pine Street house,—dating well from its brown decade, with the mildly incongruous architecture and the feeling of space and dignity,—the bit of a garden with magnolia and lilac bushes enclosed within the privacy of the gray stucco wall, the interior with just that note of haphazard imperfection which is only achieved when an interior is, as it should be, the shell of a human being and not the blue print of a decorator. The lounge was scattered with books and magazines, the tea trays drawn close to the warmth of the fire. Victorian glass flowers stood on the mantelpiece under a glass jar, and on the walls a colored reproduction of a Degas, some fine Hokusai and Sunsho prints, and a painting or two in old Venetian frames.

Perhaps there would turn up late in the afternoon George Luks or Rockwell Kent, John Carroll or Grosz, or any of the artist friends who were passing through for an exhibition or some jury work. Here they would meet in turn Franklin Watkins, Arthur Carles, Henry McCarter, quondam teacher and beloved friend; and on other occasions came Bill Bullitt, Paul Cret, Francis Hackett, Charlie Demuth, down from Lancaster,—or any of Adolphe's and Edith's friends.

An impromptu supper might follow with much good talk, teeming with gossip, art, personalities, and spiced, as all good talk should be, with racy metaphor and Rabelais' robust sauce to enrich the ingredients. Then came an adjournment to the studio wing, where the rich accumulation of a life's work lay scattered about. Perhaps the most complete expression of his sensitive color, his fluid painter's ease, and his penetrating eye for the inner life that radiates in all noble portraiture were the many portraits of Edith and Peter. Among his own pictures hung an unfinished mother and child by Mary Cassatt and a figure piece by Thomas Eakins, both of whom he had intimately known.

III.

BEFORE ATTEMPTING to estimate an artist's work, one must clarify the definition of art in general, for this must become a major premise for any statement about the artist in particular. Briefly, I take it that there is no inherent quality, such as beauty, in a work of art. Such qualities which we attribute to a work of art exist actually in our own minds. The object, then, is beautiful if it satisfies the aesthetic tastes of the age, or the audience. Art is a re-creation, or critique, of life, expressed in a given medium with a certain rhythm. Its value to humanity is that the work of the living artist enables us constantly to re-evaluate, mold, shape our own culture, our thought processes, our outlook on life; while the art of past civilizations in the same way gives us the clearest understanding of the intellectual contribution of those cultures to our human inheritance. There is nothing unusual or extreme in this approach. It is sufficiently in accord with that of Spengler, as expressed in his masterful introduction to *The Decline of Western Civilization*, or with that of Dewey in his *Art and Experience*. It will easily explain the antipathy I feel to most current art criticism, which is usually expressed in terms of comparison and either with exaggerated eulogy or contempt. Now to state that an artist's work is the finest in the country or that it means nothing to one, may be a reflection, flattering or otherwise, on the mentality of the critic, but it tells us nothing about the artist. Again, if an artist has any creative contribution to offer, it cannot be compared in terms of better or worse with the contribution of another artist, since the only intrinsic value of either creative vision is that it is individual, fresh, and original. This originality of vision, no matter how slight, has no common denominator with that of the approach of another, without which, of course, comparison is impossible. I should not have indulged in this digression if I did not feel it important in attempting an understanding of Borie's art.

Let us first trace his growth and influences from the Munich days to full maturity. Apart from a not unusual schoolboy skill at drawing, Borie showed no early precocity or directive intent. It is probable that at the Pennsylvania Academy he fell indirectly (through Anschutz) under the influence of Eakins. It is certain that subsequently he was influenced by the palette of the Munich School, and more especially by the art of Chase, Leibl, Menzel, John Singer Sargent, and von Lenbach. Traces of this period are seen in *On the*

Porch (in the illustrations), painted in 1905, and in some of the earlier portraits, such as that of Eckley Brinton Coxe or of Mrs. St. George Tucker Campbell. This early influence was destined to disappear. Little by little the impact of French Impressionism and very definitely that of Manet, Renoir, and Cézanne began to mold his style. This was perhaps around 1906. The following year he and Edith spent in Paris, where he met Mary Cassatt, a distant connection. It was through the charm and enthusiasm of her personality, even more than through his admiration for her work, that his style rapidly matured during these early years. For he had barely turned thirty. It is hardly necessary to point out examples of this phase of his growth. Outstanding perhaps are *Woman in Red*, *Woman in Gray*, *The Black Hat*, the very beautiful *Woman Reading*, acquired by the Pennsylvania Museum of Art, *Chorus Girl*, *Nude Combing Hair*, *Peter Reading*, and *Blonde Nude*.

During the succeeding decade the Bories took occasional trips to Europe, but it was not until 1921 that he settled in Paris, where he lived and worked until the summer of 1924. Adolphe was always sensitive, susceptible, and brimming over with intellectual curiosity. It might be expected, then, during this second period in Paris,—when there were far less portraits in the offing and consequently a far greater number of easel paintings, compositions, and still lifes,—that his work would show the influence of French Modernism. The truth, however, is rather that Borie's personality had been quietly expanding, experimenting, absorb-ing, over a period of years and that his second sojourn of rest and work in Paris gave a creative impulse to this tendency. As Francis Henry Taylor has written: "For one who was trained in the heavy brown over-tones of the Munich Academy, Borie's color is the most startling revelation. It is indeed an open rebellion against the established order, and one must wonder at the curious fact that during the period when Thomas Eakins dominated the Pennsylvania Academy of the Fine Arts, there arose in Philadelphia a group of ex-perimenters in color,—Borie, the Irishman Henry Mc-Carter, and Arthur B. Carles, to name but three of them,—who introduced into the curriculum of the in-stitution a modernism that found little sympathy among the leafy landscapists of New Hope and Chester Springs, or among the shareholders at Broad and Cherry Streets."

In the preceding paragraphs I have tried to in-dicate that during his career Borie was subjected to three deep influences, the Munich School, French Im-pressionism, and Paris Modernism. Through his eclec-tic sensitivity sometimes one, sometimes another, of these influences was dominant. But throughout and from the earliest days he was always a colorist, in-dividual, sensitive, rich.

In estimating Borie's importance many friends and critics have tried to separate the portraitist from the artist, usually deprecating one side of him at the ex-pense of the other. I believe we should think of both expressions as equally important parts of the man. We are living through an age of social adjustments and consequent emotional conflicts. Every profound or sensitive artist shows these conflicts in his work.

Borie's father was a banker of wealth and social position, dominant, wilful, and intellectually intolerant. For several years he opposed Adolphe's ambition to paint, but at the same time intimated that if the son insisted, he, the father, was in a position to let him follow such an avocation in all gentlemanly comfort and security. During the three years spent at the Pennsylvania Academy of the Fine Arts, and the succeeding three years in Munich, it never seriously entered Adolphe's mind that painting was a marketable article, an economic means of supporting one's self. It is apparent that during this happy novitiate he would follow the lead of his inclination and special aptitudes. I believe that in his case this was portraiture.

In 1905, shortly after his return to Philadelphia, the paternal bank failed and from then on the sons supported themselves. Although Adolphe had shown no particular precocity as a boy, and as a student had spent far more energy in living than in learning, he blossomed into artistic maturity while still under thirty. On his return from Munich he exhibited portraits and received immediate recognition. Commissions came easily and continued until he died. With the commissions came official reputation and prizes. He was known and almost only known as a portrait painter, a member of the National Society of Portrait Painters and later of the National Academy.

But Adolphe was essentially an artist. It is inevitable that he would grow more and more to hate the irksome side of his profession, the strain to please the sitter, to achieve the likeness rather than the life, to assume an avid enthusiasm when none was felt. And so it is true, as it is with all artists, that his commissioned portraits and *post-mortems* are on the whole the most overworked, the least colorful and the least successful side of his work. Francis Henry Taylor feels that: "His portraits, for which unfortunately he was best known, seldom quite come off, unless the subject was a particularly warm friend. Unlike Sargent and Eakins his contempt for a sitter did not reveal itself in savage caricature; the *bon mot* was off the tip of his tongue before it was on the tip of his brush; he simply lost interest and did a banal job. . . . His heart lay, however, in the hundreds of canvases which he did for his own pleasure and which were stacked deep in the Pine Street studio." Of course, then, there were moments—years—of galling irritation, uncertainty, relentless self-criticism.

One is tempted to ask why he never succeeded—for his own happiness—in economically canalizing his other gifts. Here, I believe, arose the conflict. Adolphe had been conditioned to think of art as an avocation, a privilege, much as the average business man thinks of tennis or music. Consequently the still-lifes, flower pieces, nudes, and other easel pictures became a recreation, an escape from the portraits, which were the serious business of making a living. And this other work

—despite the entreaties or hopes of his artist friends—he would not or could not successfully commercialize through galleries and exhibitions. But if this were the case, why was he not indeed privileged and happy? He was eminently successful in his profession, had always a steady means of livelihood, and could yet indulge in art for its own sake. Apart from the fact that this dual approach is never as easy for the artist as it sounds to the layman and that such a course is usually strewn with intellectual and emotional hazards, there was, I believe, a further conflict. Adolphe was profoundly interested in portraiture. He could never, then, entirely separate his work into two compartments, pot-boiling portraits and art for art's sake. Hating commissioned portraits because they seemed to involve an insincerity of approach, he was yet drawn constantly back to them by a very deep impulse. He felt that he had not solved the problem if he could not please the sitter as well as himself. Here again, I believe, the artist reflected the conflict of his age, for in another culture he might have pleased both his sitter and himself. I remember his once saying to me: "The introduction of photography will eventually do more than anything else to liberate the art of portraiture. Formerly the portrait was the only means of rendering an exact likeness of the sitter, but now it can be better done mechanically. People need only turn to the artist for something the photograph cannot give, since a fine portrait is never an exact copy of life." Many artist friends would not agree with me in preferring above everything else his non-commissioned portrait studies, but I think they would agree that in them he could express everything he had to say in painting: line, color, form, interest in human psychology or mood. Forbes Watson phrased the same idea when he wrote in the *New York Evening Post* in February, 1916: "To be a good portrait painter requires not only the rare special gift for portraiture, but certain traits of character that are at least as rare. There is no field of painting that exacts more from the artist, or more sternly exposes any trait of insincerity or triviality in his attitude toward his work. Painters who can meet the test as well as Adolphe Borie are by no means to be found on every street corner.

"Mr. Borie realizes, as comparatively few painters do at present, that the human subject of a portrait cannot be regarded in exactly the same way as an arrangement of still life. He appreciates the nature of the problem and there is no evasion in his attack on it. Any one with talent can paint a still life. To paint a portrait requires not only talent, but sympathy, insight and cultivation."

And here we approach the ultimate question of import in the estimation of an artist's work. Apart from distinction of color, aptitude for portraiture, integrity of line, and intellectual sensitivity, what constituted that individual approach, that slightly different attitude toward life, which is Borie's contribution as an artist, and which will enable the future student to enjoy a clearer insight into and understanding of our time and civilization? Here lies the crucial question.

Some months ago I happened to see, almost simultaneously, two comprehensive exhibitions of contemporary prints, the one of the Paris Modernists,—Picasso, Matisse, Derain, Pascin, Chagal, Dufy and the rest,—the other by members of the American Artists Congress. In analyzing the subject matter of the two exhibitions I established the following facts. Out of the prints by a hundred contemporary American artists, sixty-six dealt with the American scene or a social criticism of American life; eight dealt with strikes or strike-breakers; six with dust, sand, drought and floods. There were no nudes, no portraits, and only one still life. And out of the hundred not one could be said to enjoy, reflect, participate in, our inherited democratic-capitalist culture! I mean reflect in the sense that Velasquez, Goya, or Titian seems at home in his courtly life; John Singer Sargent in his British upper class milieu; Manet and Renoir in reflecting their respective upper and lower nineteenth-century French bourgeoisie.

In deep contrast to the socially critical attitude of the American group, there was not one example that I can remember among the Paris contemporaries that was preoccupied even with life, let alone the social problems of humanity! The Paris artists were interested in but one topic and that was art: art for art's sake.

Now, although Borie's work is in no sense socially critical, didactic, or satirical, at the same time it could never by any stretch of imagination be thought of purely as art for art's sake—not even his flower pieces, if they are taken in conjunction with his entire output. And I think it is necessary to have seen his memorial exhibition at the Pennsylvania Museum of Art to realize the import of that total statement. It is to me very distinctly a participation in, a reflection of, a certain social background or culture, in exactly the same sense in which Eakins, Manet, Renoir, and Sargent reflected the slightly different backgrounds of their periods.

The question of the relation of the artist to his age or background has always preoccupied me. From my own approach to art in general it becomes almost the only criterion in estimating art in particular. And on this relation hangs as on a keystone many of the fundamental problems of art: the happiness of the artist and therefore the sanity and sweetness of his art; his feeling of loneliness or frustration and therefore the bitterness or fanciful escape of his work; his wholesome functioning in his social community and therefore the rhythmic flow of his art with the other forces of his generation. As we have seen, art can be purely critical or didactic. The danger then is that it will step over into the province of the sciences, which deal with facts, whereas art is preoccupied with the *experience of an emotion*. On the other hand, art may become purely ingrown through lack of direct contact with life and eventually dry up and wither. During the generation 1905-1929, when almost all American artists were wrapped up either in art for art's sake or in social criticism, Borie was content to reflect life. Of course there were other, and notable, exceptions— among them Glackens, Luks, and Bellows. What, then, exactly is the society which Borie reflects and what is his attitude toward it?

There is often a relation, almost of cause and effect, between the artist as a man and his work. Sometimes this relation seems confused or inconsequential. But often it is so apparent that the art seems a very perfect counterpart of the man. This coincidence, if you believe it that, is at any rate satisfying, since it seems to lend to the work of art a certain integrity and inevitableness, qualities which we always associate with the creative spirit.

Adolphe, as I have said, was in every sense of the word—morally and socially—an aristocrat, a man of the world, a gentleman. He was sophisticated, sensitive, sensuous. He was very essentially part of his social background. I think all these qualities are evident in his painting. It is urbane, often robust, never violent. Though curious about life it does not impose itself upon one. It is intrigued with the shades, the subtleties, the undertones of human character; yet it never indulges in satire or caricature. It is interested in the comedy of life, but content to find it in the drawing-room, the wall-enclosed garden, or the studio. Harlem, Coney Island, Fourteenth Street, and Montmartre charmed him, but he never found it necessary to incorporate them in his work. Like any born colorist he is purely sensuous, never dogmatic in his use of color.

With him it is as unconscious and intangible as a sense of humor or a smile. He will never startle the world because he has no desire to startle. And because he rarely strives for originality, he will almost never fall into cerebrations or vulgarity.

Francis Henry Taylor quotes an article of Henry McBride's on the work of Dunoyer de Segonzac as an apt analogy to Borie's work. The comparison to me is all the more fitting since Segonzac is part of and yet outside Paris Modernism, in much the same way that Borie is in sympathy with but aloof from the contemporary modernistic currents in America. Each artist, too, is consciously traditional, yet each has been unconsciously deflected or influenced by Modernism.

"As the train made its lazy way into New England," writes Taylor, "I pondered on the wisdom of Mr. McBride's remarks. I cannot remember his exact words, but he pointed out the innate aristocracy in Segonzac's work and traced this quality back to the French painters of the eighteenth century. It was a remarkably clever analysis which showed that style in painting is a great deal more than stylishness, that it is a philosophical contentment with an established order, not in the smug sense but in the manner of gastronomic pleasure in a fine meal and an exquisite bottle. Segonzac, he said, painted as a gentleman should paint, with the subtlety and nuances of one who lived well. His is an art that is saturated with good manners and easy buoyancy rather than with the artificial unaccustomed politeness of the Bohemian. Contentment savoring the present; yet through it all the aristocrat, by virtue of his deftness and urbanity, is able to voice more quietly but just as effectively the same protest against society which his less easy colleagues scream about at the top of their lungs.

"So it was with Adolphe Borie. . . . He had done for our generation of artists what Mary Cassatt (another Philadelphian who had fled its rarefied bourgeoisie) had done for hers. But there was nothing effeminate in Borie's painting, nor was it minor in key. Beef is still beef whether it be rare or well-done, and here was an artist who did not feel obliged to give it to us, according to the current fashion, in the raw. He was at his best when he was enjoying the pleasures that were his own, the portraits of Edith and Peter, a bowl of fruit on the dining room table, a buxom model in the studio garden."

IV.

During his entire career Borie held only one one-man show, at the Folsom Galleries in New York in 1915. It is not surprising, then, that the Memorial Exhibition at the Pennsylvania Museum of Art was a revelation of the amount and variety of his work outside the portrait field. But what had escaped me during his life time was the very deft unity of the unfolded pattern. Not only the portraits, but the flowers, the nudes, the landscapes, the occasional decorative panels, seemed essential to this pattern; and the pattern itself sufficient to render in paint this individual artist's reflection of a certain cross-section or slice of his times. Is not this the final mission of the creative artist?

There are certain chronological or geographical circumstances in Borie's life which unquestionably retarded his reputation and which may have deflected his art. I have often wondered what the effect on him, his art, and his audience would have been if these circumstances had been different. These speculations may seem idle but to me they are warranted since they involve the same fundamental questions about art and artists.

Although Borie experimented all his life, he reached artistic maturity extremely young, approximately in 1905, when he was still under thirty. He had grown up under the influence of the Impressionists, while Modernism was not to hold its first important exhibition in Paris until 1911, nor in New York until 1913, when Borie first saw it. He was in a sense, then caught between two generations. As a young but mature artist he was painting in an idiom which would have been completely congenial to the intelligentsia of 1870, yet he was in no sense of their philosophy or generation. His mind was far more tuned to that of the radicals of the Armory Show of 1913. But he was already too crystallized and had the tact not to try to revamp his style to the fashion of the day. Nor is his case in any way exceptional. We all remember Arthur B. Davies' desperate and somewhat ludicrous efforts to coat his lyric Welsh romanticism with a film of French cubism. Alfred Maurer, of the same vintage, succeeded in making himself over; but he lived in intellectual loneliness all his life, which ended in suicide. Borie was of that group and generation whose intellectual sympathies all went out to the cubists, but whose integrity forced them to work in a medium which the youthful intolerance of the times often despised.

I think it is also interesting to note that between 1911 and 1929, when art was primarily interested in aesthetics, portraiture and illustration were held somewhat in disrespect. Leo Stein has told me that this fact as much as anything else was what deflected Picasso from his true course in the footsteps of Toulouse-Lautrec. Boardman Robinson and Clive Weed have both intimated to me the feeling of inferiority which, as cartoonists, they had suffered when in propinquity with French Modernism. To-day the shoe fits the other foot!

Borie's art has often seemed to me—from the point of view of its relation to Modernism—to have a significance parallel to that of Vuillard, who also lived through this movement without its affecting his post-impressionistic idiom. But here we must consider the different critical background of French and American audiences. In France there is of course a far deeper and more stable inherited cultural tradition. And so although Paris may be even more receptive to new and radical theories, yet it has far more tolerance and respect for the style of yesterday and is less ready to consign it to the cellar.

These speculations would suggest that under other circumstances Borie's reputation would have been more immediate, and that he would have been mentally happier and consequently more productive. Whether his painting would have been affected is difficult to determine. I doubt it. There is a deep serenity, an integrity, an inevitable ease about his painting.

There are few who saw much of the best work of Adolphe during his lifetime. Apart from the official portraits he had never exhibited very much of his best work, the flower pieces, landscapes, and countless studies and experiments in water color, ink, or pencil. He was extremely sensitive and never satisfied with the results of his work. He was moreover too completely the artist in his disdain of any audience or criterion except his own satisfaction and that of his peers.

The rare influence of his friendship, his warm critical appreciation and genuine love of art were not, I repeat, appreciated during his lifetime as a motive force in Philadelphia. But if in the next generation Philadelphia develops a sturdy, valid, regional art—as other centres must develop their own expression and personality to round out and amplify the many cross currents and traditions, climates and flora, vigor, pride, yearnings, and suppressed desires of our nation—then Philadelphia will owe Adolphe Borie its gratitude for the unconscious part he so generously played not only in his work but in his life.

PORTRAIT PHOTOGRAPH OF ADOLPHE BORIE

REPRODUCTIONS OF PAINTINGS & DRAWINGS
BY ADOLPHE BORIE

PORTRAITS & STUDIES

Woman in Gray

On the Porch

The Black Hat
Whitney Museum of American Art

Woman Reading
The Pennsylvania Museum of Art

Woman in Red

The French Novel
Phillips Memorial Gallery

In the Café
The Metropolitan Museum of Art

The Chorus Girl

The Irish Girl

Girl with Rhododendrons

Patricia

Study

Peter Reading

In the Garden

The Matron

Study

Head (Water Color)

Rebecca

Study of Head

STILL LIFES & LANDSCAPE

Flowers

Sunflowers

White Roses

Anemones and Mimosa

Stone Fruit
Whitney Museum of American Art

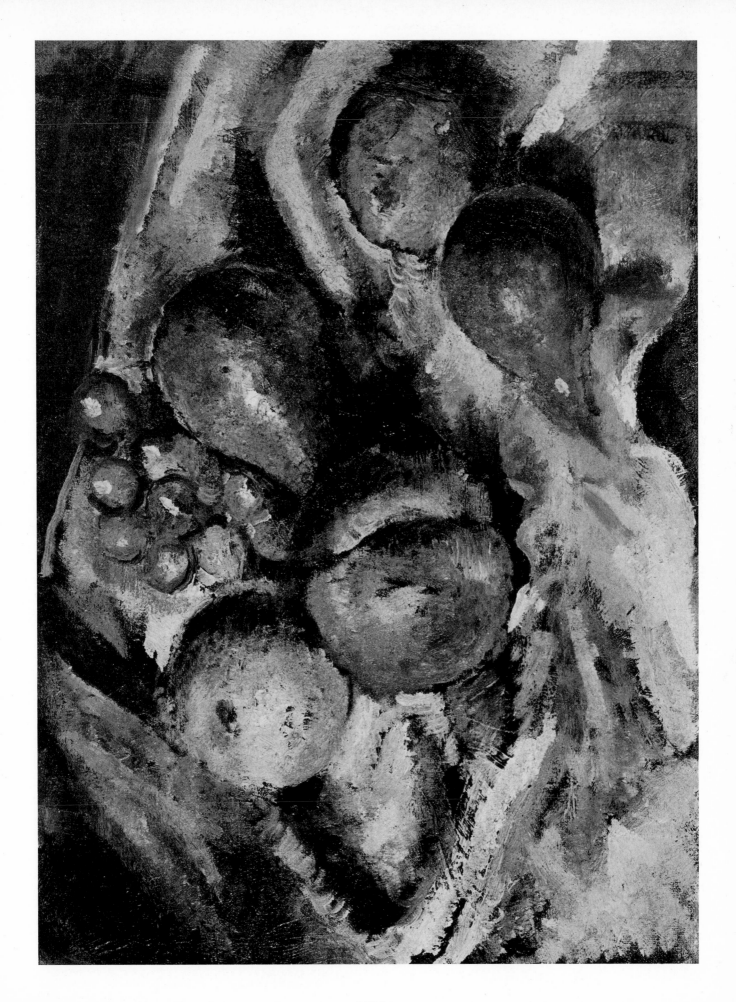

Dish of Apples

The Garden

NUDES

Seated Nude
Whitney Museum of American Art

Nude Against the Sea
Worcester Art Museum

The Blonde Nude

After the Bath

Seated Nude

Nude Combing Her Hair

The Bathers, Number 1

The Bathers, Number 2

Decoration

Nude on Sofa

DRAWINGS

Benjamin de Loache
The Pennsylvania Museum of Art

Portrait Study

Head

The Cabaret Singer

Nude

Nude

Nude

Nude

Nude

Nude